20,000 Leagues Under the Sea

JULES VERNE

Level 1

Retold by Fiona Beddall
Series Editors: Andy Hopkins and Jocelyn Potter

Pearson Education Limited
Edinburgh Gate, Harlow,
Essex CM20 2JE, England
and Associated Companies throughout the world.

ISBN 0 582 85494 6

This edition first published by Penguin Books 2005

Typeset by Ferdinand Pageworks, Surrey, UK
Set in 11/14pt Bembo
Printed in Spain by Mateu Cromo, S. A. Pinto (Madrid)

Produced for the Publishers by
Clare Gray Publishing Services Ltd, London, UK

Published by Pearson Education Limited in association with
Penguin Books Ltd, both companies being subsidiaries of Pearson Plc

For a complete list of the titles available in the Penguin Readers series please write to your local
Pearson Education office or to: Penguin Readers Marketing Department, Pearson Education,
Edinburgh Gate, Harlow, Essex, CM20 2JE.

Introduction

'Where are we?' I asked.

'On the back of the giant whale,' Ned said. Then he smiled. 'But it's not a whale.'

It is 1866. A French scientist, Mr Aronnax, wants to find a giant whale. But with his servant, Conseil, and a whaler, Ned Land, he finds a submarine – not a whale. For 20,000 leagues, the three friends stay on the submarine with its captain, Nemo, and visit many interesting places on the sea floor.

But who is Captain Nemo? Why does he want to live underwater? And how are the three friends going to escape from the submarine and go home?

Jules Verne (1828–1905) was French. His mother came from a family of boat builders and sea captains, and he always loved the sea. At twelve years old, he wanted to work on a boat in the West Indies, but his mother and father stopped him. Many years later, he had a boat and visited a lot of places in Europe on it.

Verne was the writer of *Journey to the Centre of the Earth* and *From the Earth to the Moon*. His books *The Mysterious Island* (also about Captain Nemo) and *Around the World in Eighty Days* are Penguin Readers, too.

There were no submarines or films in those days, and there was no television. But these things were all in Verne's stories. Scientists in the 1800s wanted to build submarines, but their underwater boats didn't work very well. Verne's submarine, the *Nautilus*, had answers to the scientists' problems. In 1958, an American submarine with the name *Nautilus* was the first boat at the North Pole – but this was ninety-one years after Verne's *Nautilus* went to the South Pole in *20,000 Leagues Under the Sea*.

'One small whale has a long spear on its head.'

Chapter 1   The Giant Whale

In the year 1866, a new boat came back from sea every week with the same story. 'A giant whale, a hundred metres long, came near our boat,' the men said. The story was in the newspapers and a lot of people talked about it.

'It wasn't a whale,' scientists said. 'A big blue whale is only twenty-seven metres long. Perhaps it was a coral reef.'

'But a coral reef can't send water fifty metres into the air,' the seamen answered. 'This animal can.'

It went near one boat in Australian waters. Three days later, it was seven hundred leagues away in the Pacific.

'Whales can't swim seven hundred leagues in three days,' the scientists said. 'Perhaps it's a submarine.'

But only a country with a lot of money can build a submarine, and the same answer came back from every country: 'We haven't got a submarine!'

One day a British boat, the *Scotia*, was in the Atlantic. Suddenly, water started to come into the boat. The captain looked for the problem. There was a big hole in the boat. 'The *Scotia* is very strong,' he said. 'I don't understand this hole. Is it the work of the giant whale?'

To me, a French scientist, the stories of the whale were, of course, very interesting. In 1867 I visited New York, and newspapermen there asked me questions.

'You're famous for your book about sea animals, Mr Aronnax,' they said. 'What do you think about this giant whale?'

'The sea's very big,' I answered, 'and it's the home of many thousands of animals. Scientists don't know about all of them. But one small whale has a long spear on its head. Perhaps there's a

1

giant whale with a spear, too. And perhaps this animal's spear can make a hole in a boat.'

A week later, a letter arrived at my hotel. It said:

You know, of course, about the giant whale. One day this whale is going to kill people. But we are going to kill it first. Please come and look for it with us. Our boat, the *Abraham Lincoln*, is waiting for you.

I wanted to see this interesting animal. I went quickly to the *Abraham Lincoln* with my Belgian servant, Conseil.

From New York, we went down the Atlantic coast of North and South America and into the Pacific. Week after week, all day and all night, the seamen watched the water. Conseil and I watched with them. But we didn't see the giant whale.

Only one man on the boat didn't watch the water. His name was Ned Land. Ned was a big, strong Canadian, about forty years old, and he was a very good whaler.

'You're never going to find this whale,' he said. 'It was near Japan in May, but it's now July. Where is it today? The Mediterranean? The Arctic? Who knows?'

For five long months we looked for the whale. Then the men started to say, 'Perhaps Ned is right.'

'When can we go home?' they asked their captain.

But suddenly, one day, Ned said, 'There it is! I can see the giant whale!'

The animal moved very quickly in the water. It came near our boat.

'We don't want a hole in the *Abraham Lincoln*,' the captain said. 'Let's move away.'

But our boat was slow. We watched the whale. 'It's going to hit us!' we said. But it didn't. It went under the boat, not into it.

All day we went after the whale, but it stayed in front of us.

'There it is! I can see the giant whale!'

'We're never going to kill this animal,' the men said. 'It's playing games with us.'

But at night the whale didn't move. 'Perhaps it's sleeping,' Ned Land said. 'Let's get near. Be very quiet!'

Suddenly, water from the whale's back went up into the air and rained down on our boat. Then I was in the sea.

Chapter 2   The *Nautilus*

I'm not a young man, and I can't swim well. I started to go underwater. But then there was a strong hand on my back. I looked behind me. My servant was there!

'Conseil! Why are you in the water?' I asked.

'You were in the sea and I wanted to stay with you. That's my job, Mr Aronnax,' Conseil said. 'There's a problem with the *Abraham Lincoln*. It can't come back for us. Let's swim, and wait for morning.'

Before morning, my legs stopped working. 'Go, Conseil,' I said. 'I'm a dead man, but you're young and strong. You can find a boat . . .' Then water came into my mouth, and my eyes closed.

They opened a short time later. I was with Conseil, and Ned Land too.

'I don't understand. We're not swimming. Where are we?' I asked.

'On the back of the giant whale,' Ned said. Then he smiled. 'But it's not a whale.'

I looked, and he was right. We were on a submarine!

'You and I went into the sea at the same time, Mr Aronnax,' Ned said. 'After that, I waited here. We're OK now, but this boat can go underwater. What are we going to do then?'

Suddenly, the submarine started to move. 'Quickly!' I said. 'Make some noise. Hit the boat with your hands.'

A door opened and eight men came out. We went with them into the submarine.

'Where are you taking us?' we asked the men, but they didn't answer. We arrived in a dark room. The men went away and closed the door behind them. Ned tried the door, but it didn't open. 'We're never going to escape!' he said. 'Those men are going to kill us!'

We waited for a long time in the dark room. Then the lights came on and a man walked into the room. Perhaps he was thirty-five, or perhaps fifty. He was tall, with black eyes and an interesting, open face.

In French, I said our names and asked for food and drink. He listened quietly, but he didn't answer.

'He doesn't understand French,' I said. 'You try, Ned. Perhaps he understands English.'

Ned talked in English. Then Conseil tried in German. But they had the same problem.

'What can we do now?' I asked my friends. But the man walked away and closed the door.

Again we waited. Ned was very angry. He didn't like the men on the submarine. He didn't like our room. And he didn't like waiting. 'I'm going to escape from this submarine,' he said.

A man came into the room, and Ned started to hit him in the face. Conseil and I wanted to stop Ned, but he was very strong. Suddenly, our first visitor was with us again.

'Stop, Mr Land!' he said, in very good French. 'And please listen to me, all of you. My name is Captain Nemo, and this is my boat, the *Nautilus*.

'I didn't talk to you on my first visit. I'm sorry about that. But you're a problem for me. What can I do with you? My men and I are never going back to our countries; we're always going to live on the *Nautilus*. You can live with us, too, but you can't go back

THE ARCTIC

NORTH AMERICA

EU

Atlantic Ocean

Mediterra Sea

AFRICA

Pacific Ocean

SOUTH AMERICA

At sea on the Abraham Lincoln *and the* Nautilus

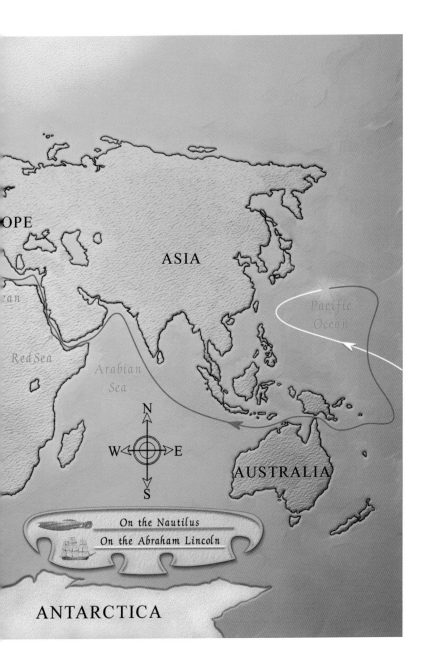

EUROPE

ASIA

Pacific
Ocean

Red Sea

Arabian
Sea

N

W ⬥ E

S

AUSTRALIA

On the Nautilus
On the Abraham Lincoln

ANTARCTICA

to your countries after that. We don't want stories in the newspapers about us.'

'What are you saying?' I asked. 'We want to go home.'

'You can go now,' he answered. 'But it's going to be difficult for you, because you haven't got a boat. You're underwater and you aren't near the coast. Stay with us now, and you can see a lot of interesting things. But you can never go home.'

Chapter 3   Our First Weeks Underwater

We stayed, of course.

We walked with Nemo's men to our new bedrooms. Then I had some food with the captain.

'Our food comes from the sea,' he said, 'and we eat very well. Our shirts, our shoes, our beds, our pens – we make all of them from sea animals, too. I love the sea! It's our only friend. People can't make problems for us here.

'But you don't want to listen to me all day. Come and see my submarine.'

We went into a room with thousands of books. 'I often read your book about sea animals, Mr Aronnax,' the captain said. 'You write very well. But your time on the *Nautilus* is going to teach you a lot of new things. A submarine is a good home for a scientist.'

I visited every room on the *Nautilus*, the first and only submarine in the seas. Captain Nemo was its builder, and he talked about his answers to the problems of an underwater boat. He was a clever scientist and a very interesting man.

Later, Ned and Conseil asked me about Captain Nemo. Who was he? Where did he come from? Why did he stay away from people and live underwater? But I didn't know the answers to their questions.

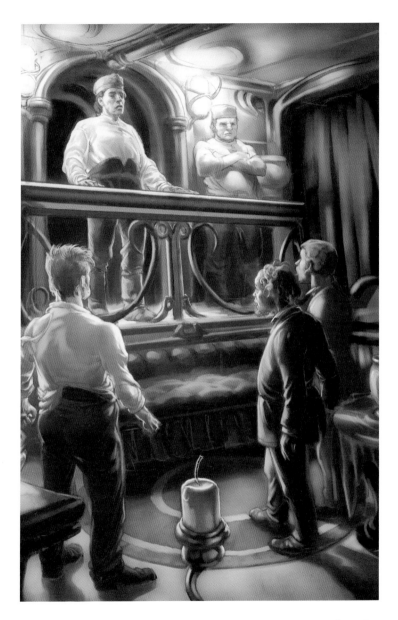

'You can see a lot of interesting things. But you can never go home.'

Then, suddenly, the *Nautilus*'s sea lights came on and we stopped thinking about the captain. The sea looked very beautiful, with fish of every colour, big and small. We didn't take our eyes from the sea all night. Captain Nemo was right: a submarine was a good home for a scientist.

The weeks after that were quiet but interesting. The submarine usually stayed about a hundred metres underwater. But every morning we went up for air, and my friends and I looked across the blue waters of the Pacific.

We didn't often see Captain Nemo. But Conseil and I looked at his books, and at the fish in the sea. Only Ned was unhappy. He wasn't a scientist and he didn't like reading. And he didn't like eating fish every day.

One day Captain Nemo said, 'There are a lot of animals in the Trees of Crespo. They make good food. Do you want to look for some with me?'

'Trees?' I asked. 'Are we near the coast?'

'They're underwater trees,' he answered.

Ned didn't want to come. But Conseil and I dressed in diving suits and walked on the sea floor with the captain and his men. It wasn't difficult. On a boat, diving suits are heavy, but they are light in the water. There was only one problem: I wanted to talk about the tall trees and beautiful fish with Conseil, but you can't hear people in a diving suit.

Captain Nemo and his men killed some big animals, and we went back to the *Nautilus* with a lot of good food.

Chapter 4   Papuan Spears

After two months on the *Nautilus*, we were near the coast of Australia. Captain Nemo wanted to take us to Asia, but the seas in front of us were very difficult. The coral reefs are famous

Conseil and I dressed in diving suits and walked on the sea floor.

because they are beautiful. But they are famous, too, because boats often hit them. There are a lot of dead seamen in those waters.

We went slowly, and looked for coral reefs under the water in front of us. For a long time we didn't have any problems. Then, suddenly, there was a big noise. The *Nautilus* stopped.

'What's wrong?' I asked the captain.

'The *Nautilus* is sitting on a coral reef. It can't move,' he answered quietly. 'But it's not a problem. After five days, the sea's going to take us away from here.'

The sea goes up and down every day, of course, and it goes up and down every month, too. Was Captain Nemo right?

Ned didn't want to wait and see. 'We can escape from the *Nautilus* today,' he said. 'The coast is near. Let's go!'

'No, Ned,' I answered. 'The Papuans live on that coast. Papuans often kill and eat their visitors.'

Every day, Ned looked across the water at the beautiful coast. 'Perhaps we can go there and look for food,' he said.

We asked the captain. 'Of course you can go,' he said, with a smile. 'Take the little boat, but be back here before night-time.'

Ned, Conseil and I arrived on the coast, and for a long time we didn't stop eating. There was a lot of fruit on the trees, and it was very good. Conseil and I looked at the beautiful animals. Ned looked at the animals, too, but he wanted them for food. He worked quickly, and that evening we had a lot of dead animals, and fruit, for the *Nautilus*'s kitchen.

We started to put things in the little boat. But suddenly Conseil said, 'Ow! What was that on my hand?'

'Look!' Ned said. 'There are men in the trees. They've got spears. They're going to kill us!'

Conseil and I were quickly in the boat, but Ned wanted to get the food first. A rain of small spears came from the trees, then one hundred men started to run to our boat. We went quickly

Ned, Conseil and I arrived on the coast.

across the water to the *Nautilus*. The Papuans stayed on the coast, because they didn't have boats.

In the morning, there were six hundred Papuans on the coast, and some of them had boats. They came across the sea to the *Nautilus*.

'We've got a big problem now,' I said to Captain Nemo. 'The Papuans can't get into the *Nautilus* today, because the doors are closed. But tomorrow there isn't going to be any air in here, because we can't open the doors. What are we going to do then?'

Captain Nemo didn't look unhappy. 'We're going to wait and see,' he said.

I didn't sleep well that night. In the morning there were a lot of Papuans on the *Nautilus*. There wasn't much air for us now, but the doors stayed closed.

'We're going this afternoon,' the captain said.

That afternoon, after five days on the coral reef, the *Nautilus* suddenly started to move. Captain Nemo was right. The sea was up – and the submarine was in water again! We moved quickly away from the coast. We looked back, and the Papuans were in the sea. Then we opened the doors, and air came into the boat.

Chapter 5   Nemo's Gold

We went across Indian and Arabian waters and into the Red Sea. Ned didn't stop thinking about escape from the *Nautilus*.

'Where are we going after this?' he asked.

'Back to the Arabian Sea first,' I answered. 'Then perhaps down the African coast . . .'

But we didn't go back to the Arabian Sea. One day Captain Nemo said, 'Tomorrow we're going to be in the Mediterranean.'

I didn't understand. 'We can't go from the Red Sea to the

Mediterranean in a boat!' I said. 'How are we going to take the *Nautilus* across Egypt?'

'We aren't going to go across Egypt. We're going to go *under* it,' the captain answered. 'I know an underwater tunnel.'

That evening, we went into the tunnel. It was very dark and very small. But Nemo was a good seaman, and the *Nautilus* didn't have any problems. In a very short time, we were in the Mediterranean.

We then moved quickly away from Egypt. Near Crete, I remembered stories in the newspapers. Crete was in Turkey, but the Cretans wanted to be Greek. A lot of Cretans were now dead, because the Turkish people were very angry with them.

I looked at the sea. There was a swimmer underwater, and he didn't have a diving suit.

'Quickly!' I said to Captain Nemo. 'Let's go to him now, or the sea's going to kill him.'

'He's OK,' the captain answered. 'His name's Nicolas, and he's a very good swimmer.'

Was this man a friend of the captain? I wanted to ask, but then I stopped thinking about the swimmer. Captain Nemo had gold in his hands! I looked behind him, and there was gold on the table, too – a lot of gold!

Later, I listened to the noises of the night. Men went away from the *Nautilus* in the little boat, and came back a short time later. Did they take gold with them? Where did they take it? Was it for the Cretans?

We didn't go near any coasts after this, and three days later we were in the Atlantic. Ned was angry. He wanted to escape to a European country, and Europe was behind us now.

But first we went up the coast of Portugal and Spain.

'We're going to escape this evening,' Ned said. 'Meet Conseil and me at the little boat at nine o'clock.'

I wanted to stay on the *Nautilus*, because it was a good home for a scientist. But I wanted to see Paris again one day, and this was perhaps the only time for an escape.

'OK,' I said to Ned.

At nine o'clock, I opened my door and started to walk to the little boat. But suddenly, the *Nautilus* stopped on the sea floor. Then Captain Nemo arrived.

'You wanted the answer to a question, I think, Mr Aronnax,' he said. 'Come with me.'

I went with him to the window. There were some old boats on the sea floor, and Nemo's men were there in their diving suits. They walked to the old boats and came back with gold in their hands.

'These boats went down to the sea floor in 1702, heavy with South American gold. My men and I sometimes come here and take a little gold. But it isn't for us. There are unhappy people in many countries. The gold is for them.'

I remembered the problems in Crete and started to understand Captain Nemo.

But Ned was not a happy man. 'Where were you?' he asked me later. 'We waited for you, but you didn't come.'

Chapter 6   To the South Pole*

A day later, we were many leagues from the coast.

'The roads here are very bad, Mr Aronnax,' Captain Nemo said. 'But do you want to walk on them with me?'

Roads under the sea? I didn't understand. But I put on my diving suit and went with the captain.

Nemo walked quickly underwater. I wanted to stay with him,

★ The South Pole, the North Pole: places in the Antarctic and the Arctic (see pages 6–7)

They came back with gold in their hands.

but it was very difficult. My feet came down on the sea floor, but the sea floor moved with me. What was under my feet?

For a long time we didn't stop walking, and then I had the answer to my question. There were old houses on the sea floor! But why were there buildings here in the Atlantic, under three hundred metres of water?

The sea floor went up. Captain Nemo stopped walking and started to write with his hand in the water: 'ATLANTIS'.

Atlantis! There were many stories about this underwater country, but for many people they were only stories. I looked down. There was a big town on the sea floor. For a long time, I didn't move. I was one of the first people in Atlantis for hundreds of years. I wanted to remember it.

After our visit to Atlantis, the *Nautilus* didn't stop. For many weeks, the sun was very strong. Then the air started to get cold and there was ice in the sea. We were in the seas of the Antarctic.

Four days after the first ice, the *Nautilus* stopped. There was ice in front of us and ice behind us.

'We can't move,' Ned said to Conseil and me. 'How are we going to escape from the ice?'

But Captain Nemo came to us and said, 'We're going to be the first people at the South Pole. We can get there in a submarine, because there's water under this ice. There's only one problem: we can't come up for air.'

The *Nautilus* went down and down. At three hundred metres, we were under the ice and there was water in front of us again. We started to move quickly to the South Pole. After a day, we were under a thousand metres of ice. But the morning after that, there were only fifty metres of ice ... then twenty ... ten ... five ... And then the *Nautilus* came up into the air and the open sea. We were at the South Pole!

It wasn't very cold – perhaps 3°C. We stayed there for three

I looked down. There was a big town on the sea floor.

happy days and looked at a lot of interesting animals and fish. Then we went under the ice again.

That night, there was a big noise. Captain Nemo said, 'The ice moved at the wrong time, and now we've got a problem. We're under three hundred metres of ice, but there's ice under us, too, and on our left and right. We're in a tunnel. But in front of us there's water, and it's going to take us up to the air.'

The *Nautilus* moved quickly in the tunnel, but then there was a noise again. There was now ice in front of us, too. The *Nautilus* started to go back. The same noise. Ice behind us.

'We're all dead!' Ned Land said.

'We've got air for two days,' Captain Nemo answered. 'After that, who knows? But there are only ten metres of ice under the *Nautilus*; under that, there's water again. We can make a hole in the ice with knives and spears, and the *Nautilus* can escape from the tunnel into open water.'

We dressed in diving suits and started to work with the knives and spears. But it was a big job – perhaps four or five days' work. And we didn't have five days . . .

After three days, we were all ill because there wasn't any new air. But we didn't stop working.

Captain Nemo worked with us. Then he said, 'Into the submarine, all of you! There are only two metres of ice under us now. The *Nautilus* is going to do our work for us.'

The *Nautilus* was strong and heavy. It went down into our hole again and again. The ice started to move, and suddenly we were in open water.

But there wasn't any air on the boat, and we were all very ill. The *Nautilus* moved under the ice. We waited and waited. I closed my eyes and started to sleep. Or was I dead?

Then, suddenly, my eyes opened. What was that noise?

'The *Nautilus* is hitting ice again, but this ice is thin,' Conseil said. 'Perhaps we're going to be OK.'

We started to work with the knives and spears.

The *Nautilus* tried again and again. First there were small holes in the ice. Then, suddenly, there was one big hole. The *Nautilus* went up into it. We weren't dead! We had air!

Chapter 7   Goodbye to the *Nautilus*

After our visit to the Antarctic, we didn't see Captain Nemo very often. The *Nautilus* went up the coast of South and North America. We wanted to escape, but every night there was a problem: we weren't near the coast, or the sea was difficult.

Then we went across the Atlantic to Europe and arrived in British waters.

Suddenly, there was a big noise: *Boom!* We looked across the sea. There was a big boat three leagues away.

'It was that boat!' Ned said. 'It wants to hit the *Nautilus* and kill us all.'

'Which country is it from?' I asked.

'I can't see,' Ned answered.

Boom! Water went up into the air only five metres from the *Nautilus*.

Captain Nemo arrived. He was very angry, and he didn't look at us. He looked at the boat across the water and said, 'First you take my country and my family, and now you want to kill me too. But can you find me underwater? No! The *Nautilus* is going to hit your boat and kill you all.'

I wanted to stop the captain, but he didn't listen to me. The *Nautilus* moved away from the coast, and the boat came after us. Then we went underwater. For a short time it was quiet. Then we started to move very quickly. Suddenly, the boat was in front of us. The *Nautilus* went into it.

There was a big hole in the boat now. A lot of water went in, and the boat started to go down slowly under the sea. There were hundreds of men in the water. Captain Nemo watched them quietly. In a short time, they were all dead.

Nemo went back to his bedroom. I looked at him from the door. He was on the floor, and in his hands there was a photograph of a beautiful young woman and two small children. His dead family!

After that unhappy day, we went up the coasts of Britain and Norway and into the seas of the Arctic. For a week, Ned, Conseil and I didn't see Captain Nemo and his men.

Then one day Ned said, 'I can see the coast. It isn't near, but I can't stay on the *Nautilus*. I want to be home – or dead in the sea.'

I wanted to be away from the submarine, too. 'You're right, Ned,' I answered. 'Let's escape this evening.'

'I'm going to put food in the little boat. Be there at ten,' he said.

At ten o'clock, I went to the little boat. Ned and Conseil were there before me.

'OK, put the boat in the water,' Ned said.

But suddenly, there were noises from Nemo's men. Did they know about our escape?

'The Maelstrom, the Maelstrom!' the men said.

This was a big problem. All seamen know about the Maelstrom. Some of the seas of the Arctic move very quickly, and in one place, two of those seas meet. There, a giant hole opens in the water. Boats and whales ten leagues away can't escape it. The Maelstrom takes them all down to the sea floor.

The Maelstrom now wanted the *Nautilus*. We looked at the big hole in the sea in front of us. 'The Maelstrom's going to kill us!' we said.

There was a noise, and our little boat went into the sea. I went in, too. My head went under the water. Then my eyes closed . . .

♦

I opened my eyes. Ned and Conseil were there. We were in the house of a Norwegian seaman.

How did we get here? We don't remember. But in a short time, we can go home. Every day we talk about the *Nautilus*. We have a lot of questions, but perhaps we are never going to know the answers. Where did Captain Nemo come from? Who killed his family? Did he and his men escape from the Maelstrom? And where is he now?

ACTIVITIES

Chapters 1–2

Before you read

1 You are going to read *20,000 Leagues Under the Sea*. Look at the pictures. How and why do the people in the story go under the sea? Talk about it.

2 Look at the Word List at the back of the book. Then answer the questions.

    a What do you know about whales? Can you see whales near the coast in your country?

    b What do you know about boats in the 1800s? Were there any submarines at that time?

    c What can make holes in boats?

While you read

3 Read the sentences. Are they right (✔) or wrong (✘)?

    a Blue whales are never a hundred metres long.   .....

    b The seamen on the *Scotia* are dead because there was a hole in their boat.   .....

    c The men on the *Abraham Lincoln* want to kill the giant whale.   .....

    d Conseil falls into the sea.   .....

    e Ned wants to stay on the submarine.   .....

After you read

4 Talk about these boats. What do we know about them?

    a the *Scotia*   **b** the *Abraham Lincoln*   **c** the *Nautilus*

5 Why are these people on the *Abraham Lincoln*?

    a Mr Aronnax   **b** Conseil   **c** Ned Land

6 What do we know about Captain Nemo?

7 Work with two friends. You are Mr Aronnax, Conseil and Ned Land. You are on the *Nautilus* and you want to go home. Talk about your problems. What are you going to do?

Chapters 3–5

Before you read

8 Talk about these questions.

   a Would you like a holiday on a submarine? Why (not)?

   b Are there any long tunnels in your country? What do they go under? Do you like going in tunnels?

   c What do you know about coral reefs? What problems can boats have with them?

While you read

9 Finish the sentences.

   a The people on the *Nautilus* can walk underwater because they put on ....

   b Mr Aronnax, Conseil and Ned go to the Papuan coast because they want to find ....

   c The *Nautilus* goes in an underwater tunnel from the Red Sea to the ....

   d Nemo's men walk to boats on the sea floor and bring back ....

After you read

10 Who are these people?

   a They want to be Greek.

   b They sometimes eat people.

   c He doesn't like living on the *Nautilus*.

   d They make their shoes and shirts from sea animals.

   e He gives gold to unhappy people in many countries.

11 You are Mr Aronnax, Conseil or Ned. Think of an interesting day on the *Nautilus* and talk about it.

Chapters 6–7

Before you read

12 The *Nautilus* is going to visit these places. What do you know about them?

   a Atlantis   **b** the Antarctic   **c** Norway

13 Are Mr Aronnax, Conseil and Ned going to escape from the *Nautilus*? How?

While you read

14 What comes first? And then? Write the numbers 1–5.

    a They see the Maelstrom.   . . . . .

    b Captain Nemo kills a lot of seamen.   . . . . .

    c They go to the South Pole.   . . . . .

    d They are very ill because there is no air.   . . . . .

    e They visit an underwater town.   . . . . .

After you read

15 What new things do we read about Captain Nemo in these two chapters?

Writing

16 You are one of Captain Nemo's men. Write about your captain. Do you like living and working with him on the *Nautilus*? Why (not)?

17 You are Ned. From Norway, write a letter to your sister in Canada. How are you? How did you arrive in Norway? Who are you with? When are you going to see your sister again?

WORD LIST *with example sentences*

air (n) Fish can't live for a long time in the *air*.

captain (n) The *captain* went to sea with fifty men on his boat.

coast (n) I love the sea, and I have a holiday on the *coast* every year.

coral reef (n) Some beautiful fish live in the *coral reef*, only four or five metres under the sea.

diving suit (n) In a *diving suit*, you can stay underwater for a long time.

escape (n/v) We can't *escape* from this room, because there are no windows.

fish (n) We eat a lot of *fish*, because we live near the sea.

giant (adj) It was a *giant* shoe, perhaps two metres long.

gold (n) You can't take that *gold* from the bank in a bag! It's very heavy.

hole (n) My shoes are very old. They've got *holes* in them.

ice (n) After rain and a cold night, there was *ice* on the roads.

kill (v) He's dead, of course. But what *killed* him?

league (n) The boat's a *league* away – about 5,000 metres.

metre (n) He's two *metres* tall.

scientist (n) Einstein was a German *scientist*.

servant (n) My *servants* do my housework for me.

spear (n) A *spear* can kill a man from twenty metres away.

submarine (n) I work underwater, on a *submarine*.

tunnel (n) There's a *tunnel* under the sea from England to France.

whale (n) There aren't many *whales* in our seas now. *Whalers* kill them, because they can make a lot of money from dead whales.